PRE-EMPTIVE ANALGESIA FOR PRIMARY TOOTH EXTRACTIONS IN CHILDREN

PRE-EMPTIVE ANALGESIA

SUNNYPRIYATHAM TIRUPATHI

Made with ♥ on the Notion Press Platform
www.notionpress.com

This book is dedicated to my loving father

Late shri Krishna tirupathi

Contents

CHAPTER ONE

Introduction

Pain, Fear, Anxiety are three dimensions which can negatively affect the behaviour of child in dental practice. Pain can subjectively evoke a sense of innate fear and anxiety, so pain control should be the main stay of any treatment protocol in dentistry especially for children. Pain should be managed pre, intra as well as post-operatively. Even if the dentist achieves excellent pain control pre and intra operatively, after discharge if the situation arises where the child has acute post-operative pain which does not respond well to analgesics, the negative feeling hampers further cooperation of the child in the successive appointments. To prevent the episode of acute post-operative unresponsive pain, methods such as administration of local anaesthesia, pre-emptive administration of analgesics, performing invasive procedures with minimal tissue damage and inflammation, preventive analgesic administration are being evaluated.

The concept of pre-emptive administration of analgesics is one of the extensive studied topic among the previously mentioned methods in the field of medicine and dentistry. Pre-emptive analgesia involves delivery of analgesic agent prior to start of surgical procedure. It is thought that by initiating analgesic interventions before surgical procedure, can mitigate intraoperative and post-operative nociception to the central nervous system and hence provide superior benefits in comparison to the same analgesic if given post-operatively. The effect of surgical injury on peripheral and central sensitisation on pain responses is already validated in the studies by Woolf [1]. It is hypothesised that peripheral and central sensitisation causes allodynia, hyperalgesia which can be mitigated by pre-emptive analgesia administration.

Pre-emptive analgesic administration in children in the field of general pediatric surgery for tonsillectomy and orthopaedic surgeries report conflicting results with a positive results in few , [2, 3] and negative results in others [4-6]. In the field of dentistry, few systematic reviews were published which were mostly reported in adults show encouraging results of pre-emptive analgesic administration for procedures such as third molar extractions [7, 8].

To the best of our knowledge no systematic review so far has evaluated the efficacy of pre-emptive analgesic administration in dental procedures in children. The aim of the current systematic review is to evaluate the efficacy and safety of pre-emptive administered analgesic for primary tooth extractions in children.

CHAPTER TWO

Materials and Methods

Protocol: This study was registered in Prospero database CRD42020206878, and followed PRISMA guidelines for reporting. Eligibility criteria: The search strategy was performed with [PICO] framework: population, intervention, comparison, and outcome, based on the following question "Efficacy and safety of pre-emptive analgesic agents for primary/deciduous tooth extractions in children". The Population Intervention Comparison Outcome (PICO) search strategy of the systematic review was: [P] population: children; [I] intervention: pre-emptively administered analgesics ; [C] comparison: no administration or preventive analgesic administration of placebo or any other active agent (analgesics administered post-operatively. [O] outcome of interest: post- operative pain, analgesic consumption, adverse effects if any.

An electronic search was performed in three databases-PubMed, Ovid SP, Cochrane. The search was conducted from publication years 1980 to 2020. The last search was performed on 1 July 2020. Articles published in English are only included. The search was based on the pre-specified question using relevant MeSH terms. Broad search was made using combination of MeSH terms (((((preemptive) OR (pre-emptive)) OR (preoperative)) OR (pre-operative)) AND (children)) AND (dental) in PubMed. Pre- emptive and children and dental in Ovid SP and Cochrane.

Eligibility criteria: Randomized clinical trials appraising pre-emptive analgesia for primary tooth extraction to that of post-operative analgesic administration (preventive analgesia) were included. Non randomized trials, comparative studies, short communications, technical notes, opinions, case reports, narrative reviews, and systematic reviews and articles that are not published in english language were excluded. Studies retrieved after comprehensive MeSH terms search were imported to citation software Zotero (www.zotero.org) from all the databases, and exclusion of duplicates was performed and then a screening of titles and abstracts was carried out. Pertinent articles were then included for a full text review. Data analysis, segregation, and recording was done by two independent authors. The outcomes evaluated were post operative pain or discomfort, side effects etc,.

Data synthesis: Qualitative analysis of selected studies was carried out.

Risk-of bias (RoB) assessment: The methodological quality assessment of the included articles was conducted independently by two review team members using the Cochrane Collaboration's criteria. Risk of bias was evaluated for all the seven parameters: random sequence generation, allocation concealment, blinding of participants and personnel and outcome assessment, completeness of outcome data, selective reporting of outcomes, and other sources of bias.

CHAPTER THREE

Results

In all the databases, 858 records were found, of which 6 were duplicates. Removing the duplicate articles, 852 records were screened by title and abstract. Full text of the 17 potentially relevant papers were evaluated, among them 11 were excluded [9-19]. (Reasons for exclusion is presented in Table-1) As a result, six studies were included in this final systematic review [20-25]. A flowchart of the search results is presented in figure-1.

Table-1: Excluded studies with reasons

Sno	Excluded articles	Reasons for exclusion
1.	Abou EL Fadl et al 2019	Pulpotomy was the procedure evaluated
2.	Veneva et al 201	Pre-emptive laser analgesia for restorative treatments in children
3.	Shafie et al 2018	Pulpectomy was the procedure evaluated
4.	Mc cann 2017	Review article
5.	Keles and kocaturk 2017	Anaesthetic pre-medication hence excluded
6.	Ashley et al 2016	Preoperative analgesics for additional pain relief in children and adolescents having dental treatment
7.	Peltz et al 2012	Review article
8.	Ashley et al 2012	Review article
9.	Hosey et al 2009	Anaesthetic pre-medication hence excluded
10.	Marshall et al 2008	Anaesthetic pre-medication hence excluded
11.	Gazal and Mackie 2007	Post operatively administered analgesics

Excluded studies with reasons

Figure-1: Flowchart of selected studies

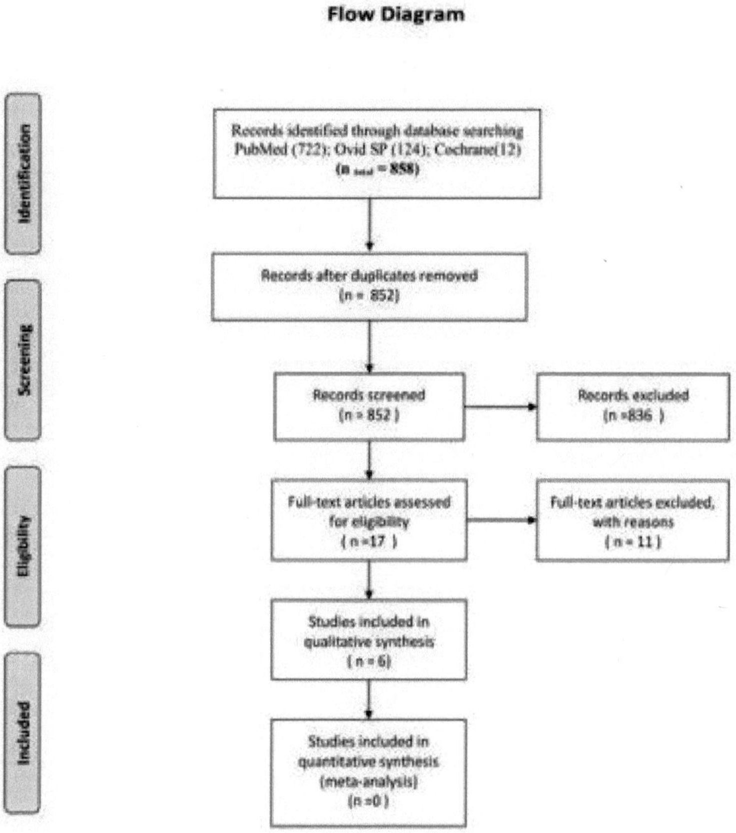

Flow Diagram

Identification

Records identified through database searching PubMed (722); Ovid SP (124); Cochrane(12) (n_{total} = 858)

Records after duplicates removed (n = 852)

Screening

Records screened (n = 852)

Records excluded (n =836)

Eligibility

Full-text articles assessed for eligibility (n =17)

Full-text articles excluded, with reasons (n = 11)

Included

Studies included in qualitative synthesis (n = 6)

Studies included in quantitative synthesis (meta-analysis) (n =0)

Flow chart of studies

Characteristics of included studies: The characteristics of the included studies are presented in Table- 2. All the six studies included were published between the years 1995 to 2020, all the studies (except the study by O'Donnell et al 1995) followed randomized design. The study by O'Donnell et al 1995 did not follow randomization, as it was multi-centre trial each centre followed specific drug protocol.

Table-2: Characteristics of Included studies.

Sno	Author-year	Study design	Sample characteristics	Procedure	Study drug administered/route/dose	Compared drug/route/dose	Follow up duration	Anxiety/ childs behaviour	Post-operative pain	Rescue medication	Adverse effects
1.	Santos et al 2020	Randomized controlled trial Triple blinded	48 children(age 5-10 years) undergoing primary molar extractions	Primary molar extraction under local anesthesia \.	Oral preemptive paracetamol 1 hour before the procedure. Oral preemptive ibuprofen one hour before	Oral preemptive saline	24 hours postoperatively after extraction	Venham's Behavior Rating Scale (VBRS) was used to evaluate the child's global behaviour during dental care. The Brazilian version of the Dental Anxiety Scale (DAS) scale was administe re d to evaluate parental anxiety	100mm Visual Analog Scale (VAS) score was measured. Mean (SD) VAS scores were 16.88 (24.07), 9.06 (19.17), and 6.25 (22.39) at 2, 6, and 24 hours, respectively, in the placebo group. In the paracetamol group, the mean (SD) VAS scores were 13.06 (23.49), 4.81 (7.99), and 1.75 (5.06) at 2, 6, and 24 hours. Finally, in the ibuprofen group, the mean VAS scores were 6.50 (12.14), 5.88 (10.07), and 1.38 (3.86) at 2, 6, and 24 hours, respectively. Multiple linear regression for covariates associated with post-operative pain at 2, 6, and 24 hours of follow-up showed that pre-emptive analgesia did not have a significant effect on post-operative pain at any time, nor the other variables investigated (P > .05).	The number of patients who used analgesics at 2 hours of follow-up was significantly higher in the placebo group (37.5%) compared to the paracetamol (18.7%) and ibuprofen (6.2%) group (P = .031).	at 2 hours of follow-up, one patient from paracetamol group and two patients from ibuprofen group were reported by their caregiver to have post- operative bleeding and swelling, respectively. At 24 hours, three patients were reported to have swelling (2 from placebo group and 1 from ibuprofen), two patients had post-operative bleeding (1 from paracetamol group e 1 from ibuprofen), one patient from ibuprofen group had fever (38.9°C), another patient from ibuprofen group reported headache, and finally, one patient from paracetamol group presented one episode of vomiting

2.	Kharo uba et al 2018	Randomized double blind control trial	105 children aged 5-12 years,	Extraction of primary tooth under local anesthesia and nitrone oxide sedation	Thirty minutes prior to their dental treatm local anesthesia a three oral liquid solutions: 15 mg /kg of paracetamo l) fruit flavored, orange color; 15 mg/kg ibuprofen	Placebo	24 hours post-operatively	Pain behavior scores were evaluated by dental assistant according to the Taddio scale was recorded before treatment, after local anesthetic and after extraction	Written and verbal instructions for post-treatment were provided to parents. They were instructed to record their children's report of pain intensity at four and 24 hours following the procedure; and to administer pain medication as needed. The children's self- reported pain-score (Wong– Baker FACES scale) and the need for analgesics at four hours and 24 hours postoperative were elicited from the parents by telephone. No significant difference reported.	Parents reported administering an analgesia within four hours following the procedure to 9/43 (20.9%), 2/33 (6.1%) and 12/29 (41.4%) of the children in the paracetamol, ibuprofen and placebo groups, respectively. The difference between the placebo and between the ibuprofen and paracetamol groups was statistically significant (p=0.004). No statistically significant was found between the paracetamol and ibuprofen groups	None reported.
3.	Baygi n et al 2011	Double blind randomised control trial	45 children aged 6-12 years	Primary mandibular molar tooth extraction under local ane	Oral ibuprofen and oral paracetamol	Flavoured placebo	24 hours	-	Five point face scale was used to record pain. unpleasantness or affective dimension of a child's pain experience. The usage of pre-emptive analgesics (ibuprofen, paracetamol) showed significantly lower pain scores compared to placebo (P < 0.05) at 15 min, 1, 2, 3, 4, 5,6 h, and 24 h. Additionally, ibuprofen exhibited	Not mentioned.	Lip bititng (n=2) and post operative bleeding(n=1) were few side effects reported in this study.

				sthesia					lower pain scores ($P < 0.05$) compared to paracetamol at the 15-min ($P < 0.001$) and 4-h ($P < 0.009$) periods.		
4.	O donell et al 2007	Multicentre randomised double blind controlled trial.	210 children aged 3-12 years undergoing extraction	Primary tooth extraction under general anesthesia	Oral paracetamol 30 minutes before procedure. Rectal volterol 2 minutes before extraction	No preemptive agent	Not mentioned	Not evlutaed	The Wong and Baker Pain Scale (WBPS) was used to evaluate self reported pain by the child. Children receiving pre emptive rectal voltarol or oral paracetamol experienced significantly less pain than no preemptive analgesia group	Not evaluated	Not reported
5.	Primo sch et al 1995	Double blind randomized control trial.	60 children aged 2-10 years.	Extraction of primary tooth under local anesthesia	Oral preemptive ibuprofen or acetaminophen	Placebo flavoured	7 hour period following surgery.	Not evaluated	No significant difference between pre-emptive and placebo group in terms of post operative pain in the first seven hours post-operatively. Pain present or absent is evaluated but quantification of pain was not done	The prevalence of postoperative analgesic usage according to test solution group was reported as ibuprofen (20%), acetaminophen (15%), and placebo (20%). No significant difference in the amount of analgesics consumption between pre-emptive and placebo group in terms in the	None reported.

										first seven hours post-operatively	

Risk of Bias: Risk of bias (figure-2) was evaluated according to Cochrane guidelines. Randomization, allocation concealment, blinding of participants, personnel and blinding of outcome evaluation is mentioned in five studies ([20-23, 25]), and is not clear in the study by O Donnell et al 2005[24]. Attrition bias and selective reporting bias is not reported in any study. Other bias (unequal distribution of study participants) was reported only in the study by kharouba et al 2019[21].

Figure-2: Risk of Bias Summary

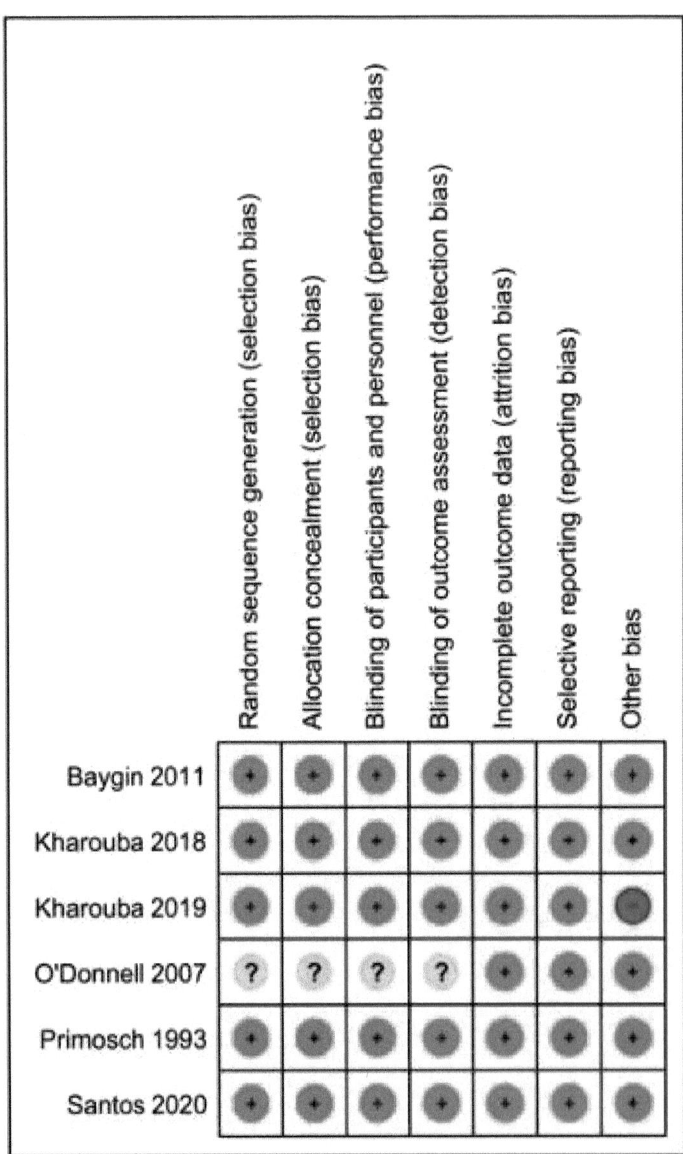

Enter Caption

CHAPTER FOUR

Discussion

All the six studies included for the final review, four studies followed double blind design[21-23, 25], study by Santos et al 2020 followed triple blind design[20], blinding was not performed in the study by O Donnell et al 1995[24]. The age of the children reported in included studies was between 2 to 12 years. Present systematic review evaluated the efficacy and safety of pre-emptive analgesic agents for primary/deciduous tooth extractions in children. Most of the included studies (n=5) evaluated primary tooth extractions only[20, 21, 23-25], except the study by kharouba et al 2017 where it was mentioned that procedures of rehabilitation such as restorations, stainless steel crowns and space maintainer placement was performed. This study was included by assuming that extractions were performed under general anaesthesia before the placement of space maintainers[22]. Primary tooth extractions were performed under local anesthesia in the studies by Santos et al 2020,baygin et al 2011,primosch et al 1995[20, 23, 25], under local anesthesia and conscious sedation in the study by kharouba et al 2018[21], under general anaesthesia in the study by kharouba et al 2017,O Donnell et al 2007[22, 24].

Pre-emptive drugs: In all the six included studies paracetamol and ibuprofen were used as pre-emptive analgesic medication [20-25]and were compared to placebo. The study by O Donnell et al 2007, used Diclofenac sodium as pre-emptive analgesic in children and compared it with paracetamol. Route of administration: Oral in the studies by Santos et al 2020,Kharouba et al 2018, baygin et al 2011,O Donnell et al 2007,Primosch et al 1995 , Intravenous administration in the study by Kharouba et al 20117, Rectal administration in the study by O Donnell et al 2007. Protocol of pre-emptive analgesic administration: Paracetamol and Ibuprofen orally administered fifteen minutes in the study by Primosch et al 1995, Kharouba et al 2017, thirty minutes before procedure in the studies by O Donell et al 2007 to one hour before the start of surgical procedure in the study by Santos et al 2020. Time of administration was not mentioned in the studies by Kharouba et al 2018 and Baygin et al 2011. Follow- up duration: Follow-up duration was not mentioned in the study by O Donell et al 2007, and it was 7 hours post-operatively in the study by Primosch et al 1995, 24 hours follow up post operatively in the rest of studies (n=4)[20-23].

Behaviour of child during, the procedure was evaluated in the studies by Santos et al 2020, Kharouba et al 2018[20, 21]. Venham behaviour rating scale was used to assess the child behaviour during treatment in the study by santos et al 2020, taddio behaviour scale was used in the study by Kharouba et al 2018.

Post-operative pain: Self reported post-operative pain was evaluated in five studies(n=5)[20-24].the study by Primosch et al 1995 did not quantify the self reported pain by the child, only presence or absence of pain was noted[25]. Scales used for quantifying self reported pain by the children were visual analog scale (VAS) in the study by Santos et al 2020[20], visual analog scale of faces (VASOF) in the study by kharouba et al 2017[22], Wong baker faces pain scale (WB-FPS) in the studies by kharouba et al 2018 and O Donnell et al 2007[21, 24], Five point face scale in the study by Baygin et al 2011[23].

Out of five studies that evaluated self reported post operative pain after extraction, three studies reported significantly lower pain scores in the 24 hour post operative period than placebo [22-24]. Two studies did not report any significant difference between pre-emptive analgesia group and placebo group [20, 21]. Mixed results might be due to differences in the methodology among the studies and also because of the reason that children cannot report pain accurately, and also the condition of primary teeth before extraction, number of primary teeth undergoing extraction also can influence the pain of the child. Multiple regression model for analysis of pain was only performed in the study by Santos et al 2020, whereas other studies did not evaluate the same so the quality of obtained results can vary.

Rescue analgesic medication: The mean rescue analgesic consumption was evaluated in four studies[20-22, 25]. Majority of the studies reported that mean rescue analgesic consumption was significantly lower in pre-emptive analgesic group than in placebo group [20-22] for 24hour post operative period. The study by Primosch et al 1995 did not find any significant difference between pre- emptive analgesic group and placebo group for seven hours post-operative period. The reason might be due to the following- shorter post-operative follow up period (7 hours post-operatively compared to 24 hour post-operative period in other studies), also there is a flaw in the pre-emptive analgesic administration : the drugs were administered based on age rather than on weight basis, also drugs were administered orally only 15 minutes before the extraction (the objective of pre-emptive administration is to achieve peak plasma levels of the analgesic drug just before the start of surgery, oral administration should be done 30 minutes or one hour before start of extractions). Side effects of pre-emptive analgesic drugs: No major adverse effects were reported in any of the included study, Some of the minor side effects reported were post-operative bleeding which stopped spontaneously, vomiting, headache, swelling, fever [20-23].

CHAPTER FIVE

Limitations of this review

following few are the limitations about this review

1. Most of the studies included children with a age range from 2-12 years, children especially younger age group children (< 4 years) cannot sufficiently describe pain unlike adults. so self reported pain scores are less reliable especially for this age groups.
2. State and stage of primary tooth (symptomatic or asymptomatic; mobile or firm, resorbed or partially resorbed or un-resorbed; presence or absence of pus) before extraction, type of primary tooth (primary incisor or primary molar) also can influence pain related behaviour which was not mentioned in the included studies.
3. Behaviour/anxiety traits of child and parent, also can influence the pain report of the child. These were also not standardised in the included studies.
4. Differences in the alertness also can differ between child who undergone extractions under general anaesthesia in comparison to children undergone extraction under local anaesthesia which also can affect the pain reporting.

CHAPTER SIX

Directions for future research

Properly designed randomized trails are lacking in this area, standardising and matching the type of tooth, state and stage of primary tooth to be extracted , standardisation of pre-emptive drugs administration protocol, comparing various routes (Oral with IV), comparison of various drugs that are deemed to be safe in children, age and anxiety matching can be performed for primary tooth extractions can be valuable research for the future. Comparison between pre-emptive and preventive analgesic administration via different routes (oral, IV); (pre-emptive versus preventive, pre-emptive and preventive) in Pediatric population is also a valuable research topic in our opinion.

CHAPTER SEVEN

Conclusions

Based on above discussion following conclusions can be made. Pre-emptive analgesic administration might have a positive effect on post-operative pain reduction and can reduce mean rescue analgesic medication taken due to primary tooth extraction in children, but the amount of evidence available to justify the same is very less. More number of properly designed and executed randomized control trials are needed to verify the same.

CHAPTER EIGHT

References

1. Woolf CJ. Evidence for a central component of post-injury pain hypersensitivity. Nature.1983; 306(5944): 686-8.
2. Abdel-Ghaffar HS, Abdel-Wahab AH, Roushdy MM, Osman AMM. [preemptive nebulized ketamine for pain control after tonsillectomy in children: Randomized controlled trial]. Rev Bras Anestesiol.2019; 69(4): 350-7.
3. Mahgoobifard M, Mirmesdagh Y, Imani F, Najafi A, Nataj-Majd M. The analgesic efficacy of preoperative oral ibuprofen and acetaminophen in children undergoing adenotonsillectomy: A randomized clinical trial. Anesth Pain Med.2014; 4(1): e15049.
4. Lee IH, Sung CY, Han JI, Kim CH, Chung RK. The preemptive analgesic effect of ketorolac and propacetamol for adenotonsillectomy in pediatric patients. Korean J Anesthesiol.2009; 57(3): 308-13.
5. Kim DH, Kim N, Lee JH, Jo M, Choi YS. Efficacy of preemptive analgesia on acute postoperative pain in children undergoing major orthopedic surgery of the lower extremities. J Pain Res.2018; 11: 2061-70.
6. Song IK, Park YH, Lee JH, Kim JT, Choi IH, Kim HS. Randomized controlled trial on preemptive analgesia for acute postoperative pain management in children. Paediatr Anaesth.2016; 26(4): 438-43.
7. Cetira Filho EL, Carvalho FSR, de Barros Silva PG, Barbosa DAF, Alves Pereira KM, Ribeiro TR, et al. Preemptive use of oral nonsteroidal anti-inflammatory drugs for the relief of inflammatory events after surgical removal of lower third molars: A systematic review with meta-analysis of placebo-controlled randomized clinical trials. J Craniomaxillofac Surg.2020; 48(3): 293-30
8. Falci SGM, Lima TC, Martins CC, Santos C, Pinheiro MLP. Preemptive effect of dexamethasone in third-molar surgery: A meta-analysis. Anesth Prog.2017; 64(3): 136-43.
9. Abou El Fadl R, Gowely M, Helmi M, Obeid M. Effects of pre-emptive analgesia on efficacy of buccal infiltration during pulpotomy of mandibular primary molars: A double-blinded randomized controlled trial. Acta Odontol Scand.2019; 77(7): 552-8.
10. Veneva E, Raycheva R, Belcheva A. Efficacy of erbium-doped yttrium aluminium garnet for achieving pre-emptive dental laser analgesia in children: A study protocol for a randomized clinical trial. Medicine (Baltimore).2018; 97(51): e13601.
11. Shafie L, Esmaili S, Parirokh M, Pardakhti A, Nakhaee N, Abbott PV, et al. Efficacy of pre- medication with ibuprofen on post-operative pain after pulpotomy in primary molars. Iran Endod J.2018; 13(2): 216-20.
12. McCann C. Preoperative analgesia for children and adolescents to reduce pain associated with dental treatment. Evid Based Dent.2017; 18(1): 17-8.
13. Keles S, Kocaturk O. The effect of oral dexmedetomidine premedication on preoperative cooperation and emergence delirium in children undergoing dental procedures. Biomed Res Int.2017; 2017: 6742183.
14. Ashley PF, Parekh S, Moles DR, Anand P, MacDonald LC. Preoperative analgesics for additional pain relief in children and adolescents having dental treatment. Cochrane Database Syst Rev.2016(8); Cd008392.
15. Peltz ID. Evidence lacking to determine whether preoperative analgesic use reduces post dental treatment pain for children. Evid Based Dent.2012; 13(4): 104.
16. Ashley PF, Parekh S, Moles DR, Anand P, Behbehani A. Preoperative analgesics for additional pain relief in children and adolescents having dental treatment. Cochrane Database Syst Rev.2012(8); Cd008392.

17. Hosey MT, Asbury AJ, Bowman AW, Millar K, Martin K, Musiello T, et al. The effect of transmucosal 0.2 mg/kg midazolam premedication on dental anxiety, anaesthetic induction andpsychological morbidity in children undergoing general anaesthesia for tooth extraction. Br Dent J.2009; 207: E2; discussion 32-3.
18. Gazal G, Mackie IC. A comparison of paracetamol, ibuprofen or their combination for pain relief following extractions in children under general anaesthesia: A randomized controlled trial. Int J Paediatr Dent.2007; 17(3): 169-77.
19. Marshall WR, Weaver BD, McCutcheon P. A study of the effectiveness of oral midazolam as a dental pre-operative sedative and hypnotic. Spec Care Dentist.1999; 19(6): 259-66.
20. Santos PS, Massignan C, de Oliveira EV, Miranda Santana C, Bolan M, Cardoso M. Does the pre-emptive administration of paracetamol or ibuprofen reduce trans- and post-operative pain in primary molar extraction? A randomized placebo-controlled clinical trial. Int J Paediatr Dent.20 30(6):782-90.
21. Kharouba J, Ratson T, Somri M, Blumer S. Preemptive analgesia by paracetamol, ibuprofen or placebo in pediatric dental care: A randomized controlled study. J Clin Pediatr Dent.2019; 43(1):51-5.
22. Kharouba J, Hawash N, Peretz B, Blumer S, Srour Y, Nassar M, et al. Effect of intravenous paracetamol as pre-emptive compared to preventive analgesia in a pediatric dental setting: A prospective randomized study. Int J Paediatr Dent.2018; 28(1): 83-91.
23. Baygin O, Tuzuner T, Isik B, Kusgoz A, Tanriver M. Comparison of pre-emptive ibuprofen, paracetamol, and placebo administration in reducing post-operative pain in primary tooth extraction. Int J Paediatr Dent.2011; 21(4): 306-13.
24. O'Donnell A, Henderson M, Fearne J, O'Donnell D. Management of postoperative pain in children following extractions of primary teeth under general anaesthesia: A comparison of paracetamol, voltarol and no analgesia. Int J Paediatr Dent.2007; 17(2): 110-5.
25. Primosch RE, Antony SJ, Courts FJ. The efficacy of preoperative analgesic administration for postoperative pain management of pediatric dental patients. Anesth Pain Control Dent.1993; 2(2): 102-6.

Printed by Libri Plureos GmbH in Hamburg,
Germany